Wrestling
Greats

# DIAMOND DALLAS PAGE

**Ross Davies**

The Rosen Publishing Group, Inc.
New York

Published in 2002 by The Rosen Publishing Group, Inc.
29 East 21st Street, New York, NY 10010

Copyright © 2002 by The Rosen Publishing Group, Inc.

First Edition

**Library of Congress Cataloging-in-Publication Data**

Davies, Ross.
Diamond Dallas Page / Ross Davies.— 1st ed.
p. cm. — (Wrestling greats)
Includes bibliographical references (p. ) and index.
ISBN 0-8239-3493-4 (lib. bdg.)
1. Page, Diamond Dallas, 1949– —Juvenile literature.
2. Wrestlers—United States—Biography—Juvenile literature. [1. Page, Diamond Dallas, 1949–. 2. Wrestlers.]
I. Title. II. Series.
GV1196.D52 D38 2001
796.812'092—dc21

                                                2001001850

Manufactured in the United States of America

# Contents

When it comes to wrestling, Diamond Dallas Page has seen and done it all.

# Ahead of Schedule

I n Diamond Dallas Page's mind, the clock was still ticking. And the pages of the calendar were still turning. The target year was 2001—ten years from the very day when he had made his professional wrestling debut.

"It's going to take you ten years," wrestler Scott Hall had told him when Page asked how long it would take for him to become a top wrestler.

"It'll take me half that," Page had responded.

DDP had already proven Hall wrong. In 1998, he had been second runner-up for *Pro Wrestling Illustrated*'s Wrestler of the Year. Twice, he had been third runner-up for Most Popular Wrestler of the Year. In 1997, his battle against Randy Savage was named Feud of the Year. It was obvious that by any measure, DDP had become a top guy in the sport.

However, the problem was that Page wasn't willing to settle for being one of the top guys. He wanted to be *the* top guy. And that meant winning the World Championship Wrestling (WCW) world heavyweight title.

So, on April 11, 1999, during the Spring Stampede pay-per-view event in Tacoma, Washington, DDP stepped into the ring against world champion Ric Flair, Hollywood Hogan, and Sting for a four-way title match. The special referee for the match was Randy Savage, Page's former enemy.

Though other opportunities to win the world title had eluded Page, he wasn't going to let this chance get away easily. As soon as the opening bell rang, Page came out fighting and went after Hogan with relish. Within minutes, Page had Hogan caught in a figure-four leglock—a painful submission hold in which the attacker hooks up his victim's legs, placing extreme pressure on the lower back and thighs.

Page and Sting lock up as Ric Flair spars with "Hollywood" Hulk Hogan during a four-way title match in Tacoma, Washington, in April 1999.

Hogan submitted, leaving Page to fight it out with Sting and Flair.

The battle wore on. Late in the match, Sting sent Page sprawling on the mat after a scorpion death lock. Page couldn't move. Then, Flair went after Sting and caught his opponent in a figure-four leglock. It looked as if Flair was about to retain his world title. However, Savage hated Flair, and there was no way he was going to let the champion get his way.

Savage climbed to the top rope and flew off of the turnbuckle, landing his elbow in Flair's midsection. Now all three wrestlers were on their backs. Savage started to count to twenty. At the count of nine, Page rose to his feet. He looked around, then executed his favorite finishing maneuver—the Diamond cutter—onto Flair. Quickly he moved in to make the cover. Savage made the three count. Diamond Dallas Page had won his first WCW world championship.

The crowd was stunned. For years, Page had been the white knight of WCW, refusing to take advantage of others' misfortune and always fighting against the rulebreaking elements in the federation. This time, Page had taken advantage of Savage's misdeed.

"Six months ago, DDP wouldn't have made the pin, but fair play never got me anywhere, so I took advantage of

Diamond Dallas Page raises the WCW world title belt in victory.

the situation," Page said. "Let those two hotheads fight it out, Jack. I got the belt, and that's all that matters."

Eight years after making his ring debut, DDP was on top of the world. As a child, injuries had stopped him from playing hockey. In college, boredom with school had stopped him from playing basketball. But nothing could stop him from wearing wrestling's gold belt.

# 2 A Diamond in the Rough

**D**on't be fooled by the name "Diamond" Dallas Page. There were neither diamonds nor vast riches in Dallas Page's childhood. And yet, the child—born Page Falkinburg on April 5, 1949—who hailed from Point Pleasant on the New Jersey coast, was truly a diamond in the rough. He was a kid who had every right to turn into one of life's forgotten losers, but instead, he became a big winner.

Page Falkinburg was born to Sylvia Falkinburg and Page S. Falkinburg, who was called Page One. Their son was "Little" Page. Little Page was the oldest of three children. A brother, Rory, was born eighteen months later, and their sister, Sally, was born a year after that.

Little Page's parents had a rocky relationship that affected their children. Page One was a drinker who, though he loved his children, spent very little time at home. Sylvia was a hard worker who did her best to keep her family together. Page One and Sylvia had frequent breakups, and they finally divorced when Little Page was three.

Little Page was a handful. He was rambunctious, and he was always getting into trouble. For a while, the three children lived with their grandparents, and there were times when the kids were housed by family friends. Finally, Rory and Sally went to live with their mother, while Page went to live with his father.

Eventually, Page's father got remarried. Little Page's stepmother, Elsie Hill, acted like a mother to him. Father and son had a close relationship. They loved watching football together. Page One was a New York Giants fan and Little Page became a Dallas Cowboys fan—thus, his lifelong nickname: Dallas.

Unfortunately, Page One couldn't sit still. Once again, he had difficulty handling the responsibilities of being a husband and a father. Little Page was eight when his father left home for the last time. They would see each other only a few times during the next ten years. After his father left home, Dallas moved in with his grandmother, Doris Seigel, in Point Pleasant, New Jersey. His mother visited him on weekends.

Living with his Grandma Doris provided Little Page with some long-awaited stability. His grandmother was a disciplinarian who demanded that all of her grandchildren go to school and behave well. While living with his grandmother, Page also got his first taste of professional wrestling. The family watched a lot of wrestling at Grandma Doris's house, and Page took an instant liking to the bad guys. As a troublemaker, he could relate to them easily.

Like most children, Page had a lot of likes and dislikes. As it turned out, he wasn't very good in school. Although he was an enthusiastic student, Page had a hard time reading and didn't have the patience to study. He hid his troubles with reading from his teachers and devised cheat sheets for tests. However, Little Page loved sports and played in youth football and hockey leagues. Page became a very good ice hockey player.

Unfortunately, Page never got the chance to find out how far he could go with his hockey and football skills. On a winter morning when he was twelve, Page's trip to the candy store ended up changing his life. That morning, as Page was crossing the street near the bus stop, he looked over his shoulder to ask a friend if he wanted anything from the store. The next thing he knew, Little Page was flying through the air. His friend had screamed, but it was too late. Page was struck by a car.

"I didn't feel the car's impact until I woke up on the ground," an older Page later recalled.

The accident changed his life. Little Page went from being an active and rambunctious kid to being confined to his bed. Doctors told him that if he kept on playing contact sports, he'd need a cane to walk by the time he was forty. So, after a long period of rehabilitation, Page found another sport to keep him occupied: basketball.

As it turned out, Page was perfectly suited for hoops. He was taller than most other kids his age (and would grow up to be six feet five). At first, Page wasn't very good at basketball, but because he liked the game so much, he worked hard to improve. By ninth grade, he was a starter on the undefeated freshman team at St. Joseph's High School in Point Pleasant, New Jersey. In tenth grade, he made the varsity team. By twelfth grade, he was starting every game for the Point Pleasant Boro High School team. He was among the team leaders in several categories and was

Diamond Dallas Page, always good at hockey, football, and basketball, was a natural in the wrestling ring.

named to the All-Ocean County team. He was so good that small colleges were trying to recruit him.

Since Page wasn't a good student, high school and college were merely a means to an end: playing basketball. However, it was during this period that the time and energy Page was sinking into basketball were transferred to his job at a local bar. At age eighteen, Page took his first job at Jimmy's Sea Girt Inn. Though he started out doing menial tasks like mopping floors and stocking beer, after a while, he became the bouncer. He really liked the job; after all, Page the Bouncer had no trouble attracting pretty women.

After he graduated high school, Page attended Stockton State College in Pomona, New Jersey. From there he transferred to Ocean County College, where he was an honorable mention Junior College All-American in basketball. After his sophomore year, he accepted a full scholarship to Coastal Carolina University near Myrtle Beach, South Carolina.

Even though he had a full basketball scholarship, Page was bored at school. The bar scene in Myrtle Beach had quieted down after Labor Day, and Page found himself with nothing to do when he wasn't attending classes or playing basketball. Later in the fall, he caught the flu and lost twenty pounds in three weeks. After less

> It was then that Page saw a sign on the gym wall that read, "Wrestling Tonight."

than two months at Coastal Carolina, Page walked into the gym and told his coach that he was going home. It was then that Page saw a sign on the gym wall that read "Wrestling Tonight."

The night before he headed back to New Jersey, Page attended the wrestling matches at the Coastal Carolina gym. He was intrigued by what he saw. "I can do that," Page thought.

Though the thought of wrestling intrigued him, at age twenty-one, Page wasn't really sure what he wanted to do. How could he make a commitment to only one thing? He ended up opening a business called Page's Painters. He also found the time to do some wrestling after learning the basics from Tito Torres, who ran a storefront gym in Jersey City. Eventually, however, after reinjuring his knee, Page stuck to running bars, and he did so in New Jersey, Texas, and Fort Myers, Florida.

Page was never able to forget about wrestling. Although he doubted that he could become a successful pro wrestler, he realized that there was another side of the sport that suited his personality: managing. It was at this time that the rock 'n' wrestling craze was sweeping the nation. Meanwhile, the American Wrestling Association (AWA) had just lost

Paul E. Dangerously, a flamboyant, loud-mouthed manager. Page made a tape of himself with a couple of beautiful women that he called the Diamond Dolls, and he sent it to the AWA.

At first, the bigwigs in the AWA were reluctant to hire Page. They were so impressed by his audition tape, they were afraid that Page would simply use the AWA as a springboard to bigger and better things. However, the federation was down on its luck. Television ratings were dropping, and attendance was horrible. In 1988, the AWA took a chance and hired the man who from then on would be known as Diamond Dallas Page.

# Managing to Be the Best

**D**iamond Dallas Page was where he wanted to be. He had always been attracted to action, and there was plenty of action in the AWA, even if the federation was in decline. Page became the manager of Badd Company—the team of Pat Tanaka and Paul Diamond—and set out to make them the best and most flamboyant duo in the AWA. On March 19, 1988, Badd Company defeated the Midnight Rockers—Shawn Michaels and Marty Jannetty—for the AWA world tag team championship.

For the AWA, Page was a breath of fresh air. Wrestlers such as Greg Gagne and Nick Bockwinkel, who had plenty of skill but lacked personality, had become the trademark of the federation in the late 1980s. The federation had become dull. Fans were defecting in droves to the WWF and the NWA. But DDP was different. He was brash, he was loud, and he was flamboyant. He constantly interfered in his team's matches. Thanks mostly to Page, Badd Company held the world tag team belts for over a year before losing to Ken Patera and Brad Rheingans on March 25, 1989.

However, by 1989, the AWA was operating on borrowed time, and Page was looking for a new outlet for his creativity. He found it with Florida Championship Wrestling (FCW)—a regional league that had been home to several legendary wrestlers, including Dusty Rhodes, Kevin Sullivan, Superstar Billy Graham, and Lex Luger. Page took a job as a color commentator for FCW and worked alongside famous TV announcer Gordon Solie. He even managed a few wrestlers.

Although Page was by no means a star, his life was headed in the right direction. He had a job in wrestling and a successful nightclub in Fort Myers called Norma Jean's. And in December 1989, he met the woman of his dreams: Kimberly Lynn Bacon. Kimberly, a senior at Auburn University, was in Fort Myers on Christmas break, when, one night, she walked into Norma Jean's, and Page immediately fell in love with her. Soon, the feeling was mutual. They got married on December 1, 1991, at a historic house in Fort Myers.

In the meantime, Page had a tryout with the World Wrestling Federation, but he wasn't offered a job. After Florida Championship Wrestling folded, in early 1991, Page became a manager in the National Wrestling Alliance (NWA).

Page was an instant hit in the NWA—the same as he was in the AWA.

The first team he managed was the Fabulous Freebirds. The Freebirds—Jim Garvin and Michael Hayes—were one of the most famous tag teams ever. In 1981, they were named Tag Team of the Year by *Pro Wrestling Illustrated* magazine. After their glory years in Texas, the Freebirds were considered to be on the downside of their careers. DDP changed that. On February 24, 1991, Garvin and Hayes beat Butch Reed and Ron Simmons for the NWA world tag team championship. Now Page had helped two teams win world tag team championships in two different wrestling leagues.

Shortly afterward, Page added the Diamond Studd to his stable of wrestlers.

Diamond Dallas Page mugs for the camera during a wrestling card.

The Diamond Studd's real name was Scott Hall, and he would go on to superstardom in WCW and in the WWF (as Razor Ramon). Page also brought in the Diamond Dolls, a bevy of beautiful women who accompanied him to the ring before each match.

The Freebirds lost the NWA world tag team belts, but they beat the Young

Pistols for the vacant WCW U.S. tag team title (the NWA became WCW in early 1991). Page kept interfering in his men's matches. The Diamond Studd became one of the most despised men in WCW . . . other than, of course, his manager.

Page soon realized, however, that interfering wasn't nearly as much fun as actually wrestling. Sure, his bad knee was still a major concern, but Page was willing to take a chance. He had never dreamed about becoming a manager. He had never dreamed about becoming a TV announcer. He had only dreamed about becoming a pro wrestler—and he wanted to see if he could make that dream come true.

With the backing of former wrestler Magnum T.A., Page enrolled in a wrestling school in Atlanta called the Power Plant. His teachers were Jake Roberts, the Assassin, and Dusty Rhodes. Everybody warned him that becoming a successful pro wrestler wouldn't happen overnight.

"It's going to take you ten years," Scott Hall said.

"It'll take me half that," Page replied.

Brash and confident as ever, Page surged on to his next career challenge.

# The Long Road Ahead

D iamond Dallas Page knew that if he was going to be a wrestler, he was going to have to forget about the injured knee that had stopped him from playing football and hockey, and that had ended his first attempt at being a wrestler. Since there was no way around it, Page simply ignored the knee.

Page wrestled his first match on November 18, 1991, in Gainesville, Georgia, just three weeks after he enrolled at the Power Plant. His partner was the Diamond

Studd, Scott Hall. Hall wasn't happy about being paired with a rookie, even if that rookie was his former manager. Although they lost, Page looked good in the ring.

The truth was that Page was a ring novice, and because of this, he lost a lot of matches during his first several months in the ring. He was little match for Van Hammer, Ron Simmons, Junkyard Dog, and Johnny B. Badd, who were all experienced wrestlers. Page was rarely seen on television. If you wanted to see him wrestle (and few people did), you had to go to your local arena and get there early. Usually, Page wrestled in the first match on the card.

In general, DDP's rookie year was filled with losses. WCW was his school of hard knocks. Naturally, Page talked a good game—in fact, he couldn't keep his mouth shut. But his boasting and arrogance weren't backed up by ring performance. Things soon went from bad to worse. In early 1993, Page and the Diamond Studd paired off against Shanghai Pierce and Tex Slazenger in a tag team match. During the match, Page took a stiff hit, and for the rest of the match, he could barely lift his arm. After the match, Cactus Jack, another wrestler, asked Page how bad the pain was.

"The pain was shooting through me and he knew what the problem was right away," Page said in his autobiography. "He said, 'You tore something, probably your rotator cuff.'"

As it turned out, Page *had* torn the rotator cuff in his shoulder. He would have to undergo a type of surgery that is considered one of the worst kinds for athletes. For baseball players, rotator cuff surgery often means the end of their careers. For Page, this was yet another in a long line of frustrating injuries that had threatened to keep him from wrestling.

Page had the surgery, then underwent a long period of rehabilitation—and learning. His teacher was veteran wrestler Jake "the Snake" Roberts, a former star in WCW and the WWF. Roberts taught Page not only about the physical side of the sport but about the mental aspects of wrestling: how to get ready for matches, how to psyche out your opponent, and how to think your way out of certain situations. Roberts was a pro at these things, and Page was a willing student.

Unfortunately, Page's contract with WCW had run out, and he didn't have a new one. WCW wasn't too interested in an injured wrestler who had lost most of his matches during his first two years in the ring. Then, Page did what he probably should have done all along: He wrestled on the independent circuit. He wrestled in Mexico's AAA promotion, where he was Roberts's bodyguard. He wrestled in Singapore, the Philippines, Austria, and Germany. Away from the television cameras and out of the glare of the spotlight, Page could work on becoming a better wrestler.

Finally, in late 1994, Page made his next big move. He could have signed with the WWF, but he chose to sign another contract with WCW instead. Page felt that he had unfinished business in the federation, so he signed a contract for about half of the amount he wanted. He would be starting from the bottom all over again.

Page did everything he could to promote himself. He hired a bodyguard named Max Muscle and challenged opponents to arm wrestling matches. Then there were the Diamond Dolls, who accompanied him to the ring. However, before long, there was only one Diamond Doll: Kimberly Page.

Page may have looked great in the ring, but Kimberly looked even better, and most of the fans directed their attention toward her.

Page's career started to turn at the Great American Bash on June 18, 1995. His opponent was Dave Sullivan, the offbeat brother of weirdo wrestler Kevin Sullivan. Dave was just as strange as Kevin was—he carried a live rabbit to the ring. Page's challenge was that if he beat Sullivan at arm wrestling, he'd get the rabbit. If Sullivan won, he'd get a date with Kimberly. Sullivan needed only forty-three seconds to force Page's arm to the table. After the match, Page and Max Muscle attacked Sullivan, who really didn't care. He had his date!

Page beat Dave Sullivan at the Bash at the Beach in Huntington Beach, California, in July 1995.

Page was enraged. He got even madder when Kimberly enjoyed her date with Sullivan. After all, Page hadn't been treating Kimberly with much respect. He never gave her a chance to talk, and he would force her to hold the ring ropes open for him. Perhaps jealousy fueled Page's competitive edge. Whatever it was, the following month, he pinned Sullivan in just over five minutes at Bash at the Beach in Huntington Beach, California. At Fall Brawl in September in Asheville, North Carolina, Page beat the Renegade for the WCW television title, his first championship.

Finally, after all the years, the injuries, and the struggles, Page's wrestling career had taken a turn for the better.

# 5 Down on His Luck

Diamond Dallas Page's luck was turning. He racked up several wins in defenses of the WCW TV title. Max Muscle's interference had a lot to do with many of those victories. Suddenly, DDP became a rich man: He won $13 million gambling in Las Vegas.

These two seemingly unrelated factors combined to feed Page's already large ego. Suddenly, all he cared about was wealth and his personal achievements. His on-camera treatment of Kimberly became worse. In fact, many viewers couldn't believe that Kimberly put up with Page's nonsense. He treated her like a prop: a beautiful woman whose only purpose was to make him look better.

But Page was about to find out that the old adage is true: You'll meet the same people on the way down that you met on the way up.

First, Page was pinned by Johnny B. Badd at Halloween Havoc '95 and lost the TV title. He also lost Kimberly, who had agreed to become Badd's ring valet if Page lost the match. It was the ultimate act of arrogance on Page's part. Not only did he think he was unbeatable, but he also thought he had the right to bet Kimberly, too.

"I'm tired of being treated like a possession," Kimberly said on television.

Suddenly, the losses started piling up. Page lost every rematch to Badd, including a match at the World War III pay-per-view event on November 26, 1995. Even worse, as far as Page was concerned, Kimberly seemed to enjoy being with Badd. No surprise there—Badd treated Kimberly with respect and dignity.

Although he was now losing most of his matches, Page was voted Most Improved Wrestler of 1995 by the readers of *Pro Wrestling Illustrated* magazine. That honor fed Page's ego only fleetingly.

Though he suffered a few setbacks, DDP was named Most Improved Wrestler of 1995 by the readers of *Pro Wrestling Illustrated*.

He desperately wanted to beat Badd, but he couldn't. He desperately wanted to win back Kimberly, but he couldn't do that either.

Page's fortunes went from bad to worse. He lost every penny to Kimberly when he lost to Badd at SuperBrawl '96 in St. Petersburg, Florida in February. DDP was flat broke. One night, he was seen on television trying to sell a pair of his wrestling tights. Page couldn't even afford to pay his bills. And to make matters worse, Kimberly wouldn't even look at him. On television, she stated that she preferred Badd's company to Page's. Of course, this only served to enrage him more.

Shortly after SuperBrawl, Page helped Lex Luger beat Badd for the TV title. DDP still wanted revenge against Badd, but Badd left the federation and signed with the WWF. The problem was that Page had already signed to wrestle Badd in a loser-leaves-the-federation match at Uncensored '96 in Tupelo, Mississippi. The Booty Man—also known as Brutus Beefcake—replaced Badd for the match and won. Even worse,

Kimberly contributed to Page's defeat by slapping him across the face.

Page was as down as a man could be. He was penniless. Kimberly had found a new man and was calling herself the Booty Babe. But perhaps worst of all, Page was out of wrestling. He was out on the streets, jobless, and homeless.

Of course, Diamond Dallas Page has never been the kind of man to take no for an answer. Page didn't give up. He found a loophole in his contract that allowed him to return to WCW. After all, Page argued, "I didn't sign for a loser-leaves-the-federation match against the Booty Man. I signed for that match against Badd."

Not only was Page back in action, but he was off the streets, too. Once again, he was riding around in limousines, wearing fancy jewelry and sharp-looking clothes, and enjoying the life of a rich man. Where had his money come from? Page hinted to the existence of a benefactor, but he wouldn't say who it was. The benefactor turned out to be Kimberly, although nobody knew that at the time.

Page immediately got back on the winning track. At the Slamboree '96 pay-per-view event, he pinned Bobby Eaton, Johnny Grunge, and Barbarian to win the eight-man Battlebowl battle royal and earn a shot at the world title. Page didn't make the most of that opportunity, but he piled up victories over several top-level opponents, such as Hacksaw Duggan, Eddy Guerrero, and Chavo Guerrero.

The WCW TV title remained elusive. The world and world tag team titles remained out of reach, too. Most important, though, Badd was winning big matches at spotlight events. He pinned Chavo Guerrero at Fall Brawl '96 and pinned Eddy Guerrero at Halloween Havoc. Those wins caught the attention of many wrestling fans because the Guerreros were outstanding wrestlers.

But the series of events that would have the most effect on Page's career occurred during the summer of 1996. Former WWF wrestlers Kevin Nash,

Scott Hall (formerly the Diamond Studd), and Hulk Hogan had invaded the federation and formed a new rulebreaking clique called the New World Order. The NWO shamelessly attacked and injured numerous wrestlers and began recruiting every top wrestler in the federation. Page was on their list.

As the NWO quickly found out, however, the only list of Page's that they were on was his "enemies" list.

# DDP Versus the World

The truth was that Diamond Dallas Page felt slighted by the NWO. After all, Hall used to be his friend. He was DDP's partner in his first tag team match. Page was offended when Hall and Nash formed the NWO and didn't ask him to be a member. When they finally made an offer, Page decided, "It's too late. They should have asked me a long time ago."

Of course, we should never forget that DDP is, at heart, a self-promoter. He has always known how to get people's attention. The NWO was becoming the most hated clique in wrestling. Meanwhile, thanks to the attention the NWO was garnering, WCW was becoming the most popular federation in wrestling. Television ratings and arena attendance were soaring. The only people who got any attention in WCW were NWO members and the many wrestlers the NWO had targeted.

DDP decided to be an NWO enemy.

Hall, Nash, and Hogan tried to recruit Page into their group, but DDP declined—loudly. One night, he used his Diamond cutter on Hall. Hall got revenge at Starrcade '96, when he, Nash, and Syxx attacked Page during his match against Eddy Guerrero. As 1996 came to a close, the NWO vs. DDP was the hottest feud in wrestling.

Page's loud-mouthed defiance of the NWO angered the quickly growing group even more. He helped several of the NWO's rivals, including Guerrero. At Souled Out in January, the wrestling world watched in anticipation as Nash and Hall walked to ringside and handed Page a black NWO T-shirt.

Would Page put it on? Millions of wrestling fans wondered. Page took the T-shirt from Nash and Hall and pulled it over his head. The T-shirt stretched over

DDP whips "Hollywood" Hulk Hogan across the ring in one of his many fierce contests with the New World Order.

DDP's muscular chest. But DDP wasn't going NWO. He used a Diamond cutter on Hall and tore off the T-shirt.

DDP's war with the NWO was making him the most popular man in the federation. He was a hero of the people, the man who would save WCW from the NWO invaders. On the weekly wrestling program *Monday Nitro* in late February, Page was brutally attacked by several members of the NWO, including Randy Savage, Hall, and Nash.

"The NWO was running wild and was taking control of the matches and the crowd, but, at the same time, the fans were reacting more positively to me," Page said in his autobiography. "The fans liked that I was taking a stand against the NWO. The threat of the Diamond cutter had given me a weapon that I could use against anyone. I knew they had strength with their growing numbers, but I refused to give in to them."

The stage had been set for another turning point in Page's career. Kimberly, who had been away from the ring for nearly a year, decided to rejoin her husband at ringside. She also accepted an offer to pose nude for *Playboy* magazine's celebrity issue.

Perhaps both decisions were a mistake. But, then again, how could DDP and Kimberly have foreseen the evil of Randy Savage and Elizabeth?

At Uncensored on March 16, 1997, Page was being interviewed by wrestling announcer Gene Okerlund. They were talking about Savage, whom Page complained had refused to acknowledge him. Suddenly, Savage and manager Elizabeth walked out carrying a copy of *Playboy*'s celebrity issue

"I have here a copy of *Playboy*'s nude celebrities issue," Savage said to Page. "Your wife is the centerfold. Tell me, how could anybody let their wife appear nude in a magazine?"

Page turned red with fury. Then Kimberly walked out from the dressing room covered in yellow spray paint. Clearly, Savage and Elizabeth were the

Security guards restrain DDP to prevent a ringside brawl.

culprits. Page shook with anger. Then Savage jumped DDP, knocked him to the ground, and spray-painted the letters NWO in yellow on his back.

The night ended with Page vowing revenge against Savage—and with Page and Kimberly more popular than ever.

Their feud raged on for several months. At Spring Stampede on April 6, 1997, Page used his Diamond cutter to pin the Macho Man. After the match, Savage grabbed Kimberly and threatened to hit her. However, Eric Bischoff, the spokesman of the NWO, prevented him from doing so.

Page turned up his assault on Savage. He attacked him at Slamboree '97. At the 1997 Great American Bash, Savage and

Page battled in another main event, a lights-out, no-disqualification match. Savage, as manic as ever, attacked two referees, then won when Hall interfered. A month later in July at Bash at the Beach, Page teamed with Curt Hennig against Hall and Savage. Hennig, however, walked out on Page during the match, leaving DDP in an impossible two-on-one situation.

Page was fearless. He refused to back down from the NWO. Lex Luger joined Page for tag team matches against the NWO, but trouble developed between the teammates. One night, Page mistakenly gave Luger a Diamond cutter. Another time, Luger accidentally placed Page in his torture rack finisher. A week later, Luger hit

Page with a forearm, enabling Hall and Savage to beat them.

Page and Luger seemed to be on the verge of a breakup. They even wrestled each other on *Nitro*. But when the NWO interfered, Page and Luger realized that they shouldn't have been fighting each other. They should have been fighting the NWO.

Indeed, the NWO would do anything to destroy Page. He had a chance to win the WCW TV title from Disco Inferno on October 6, 1997, but Savage's interference kept Page from winning. DDP executed his Diamond cutter on Savage, who laid motionless on the cement floor.

Page vs. Savage would be named Feud of the Year by the readers of

*Pro Wrestling Illustrated* (DDP was third runner-up for Wrestler of the Year and Most Popular Wrestler of the Year), and their match at Halloween Havoc on October 26, 1997, was a big reason why. This was a sudden death match, in which the winner would be the man who knocked out the other wrestler for ten minutes. The hated rivals battled all over the arena. Even Kimberly and Elizabeth got involved and fought each other. The crowd was whipped into a heated frenzy.

But controversy, a hallmark of the Savage-Page feud, was the deciding factor in this match, too. The referee got knocked out. Then Page's ally, Sting walked to ringside. Sting hit Page with a baseball bat. Page fell to the mat for well over ten seconds. Savage was declared the winner.

The fans couldn't believe what they had just seen. Had Sting really turned against Page? Was Sting on the verge of joining the NWO?

Their questions were answered within minutes. The man who looked like Sting was actually Hulk Hogan. And DDP had a new rival: the most famous man in wrestling history.

Hogan, by far the most experienced wrestler in this feud, successfully defended his WCW world heavyweight championship against Page. But there were other major titles to be won in WCW, and DDP

DDP gets ready to dispense some street justice outside of the ring on Hulk Hogan, who, disguised as Sting, interfered in his match.

targeted the one held by Curt Hennig, the man who had walked out on him during a match the previous summer. Hennig was the WCW U.S. champion.

Hennig held off Page in several matches until they met again at Starrcade on December 28, 1997. This was one of the best matches of the year. Hennig displayed his cunning and DDP showed off his strength and brawling skills. Late in the match, Page delivered a Diamond cutter that sent Hennig to the mat. DDP, sensing his opportunity, moved in for the cover. The referee made the three count.

DDP was now the WCW U.S. champion. And he was one step away from wrestling immortality.

# In the Spotlight

The WCW U.S. champion holds a lot of power. The belt is the second most important singles title in the federation—second only to the world championship. Wrestlers want the U.S. title not only because it puts them in line for more world title shots, but also because the belt is very prestigious.

And now, Diamond Dallas Page, who was four years ahead of Scott Hall's prediction that it would take him ten years to become a successful wrestler, had the power. Although DDP couldn't pick and choose whom he wanted to defend the title against, he could offer matches to anyone he wanted. He picked Chris Benoit, a great wrestler and a friend.

However, in professional wrestling, where, ultimately, most people look out only for themselves, "friend" is a slippery term. Page wrestled Benoit on *Thunder* on February 5, 1998. Raven—who, as Scotty Flamingo, had once wrestled under DDP—had his Flock attack Page during the match. A few days later on *Nitro*, the Flock again attacked Page. Suddenly, DDP had one less friend: Benoit, who turned against him, too.

Page's feud with Raven and the Flock replaced his feud with the NWO. Although the wrestlers in the Flock were lesser known than the wrestlers in the NWO, they were equally determined to destroy Page and take his U.S. title. At Uncensored on March 15, 1998, Page eked out a victory over Raven and Benoit in a triple jeopardy match. Shortly afterward, Page was appearing on *MTV Live* when Raven attacked him from behind and stole the U.S. title belt.

DDP was exhausted. Over the previous year and a half, he had engaged in brutal feuds with the NWO, Savage, Hennig, and now Raven. He was barely holding on to the U.S. title, winning matches in the

Diamond Dallas Page goes for the pinfall.

final seconds after getting dominated throughout. At Spring Stampede on April 19, 1998, DDP finally ran out of energy. When Horace Boulder, Hogan's nephew, hit him over the head with a stop sign, Page easily got pinned by Raven, losing the belt.

DDP had nothing to be ashamed of. For a man with a bum knee who had gotten a late start in pro wrestling, he had won the WCW TV and U.S. titles. The only reason he lost the U.S. title was because Horace Boulder interfered. If nothing else, Page had proven that it was nearly impossible to beat him fair and square. Only a team of wrestlers, or blatant interference and the use of a foreign object, could stop DDP.

And DDP wasn't ready to be stopped. Around this time, the NWO split into two halves: NWO Hollywood, with Hogan and Bischoff as the leaders, and NWO Wolfpac, with Nash in charge. Just about every wrestler in WCW was trying to join one side or the other. When asked which side he planned to join, Page's answer was simple: my side. After all, he hated Hogan, so he couldn't be with NWO Hollywood. And he hated Savage, who had joined the Wolfpac.

Nonetheless, there were occasional signs that DDP would align himself with the Wolfpac. On June 4, he teamed with Wolfpac member Lex Luger for a tag team match. The Wolfpac invited him to join the group. On *Nitro* the following Monday, the

Wolfpac offered him a red and black Wolfpac T-shirt. But Page never got the chance to give his answer. Hogan and Dennis Rodman of the NBA's Chicago Bulls attacked Page with a chair.

It turned out to be a tumultuous night for Page. He also wrestled Savage in a match refereed by wrestler Roddy Piper. Members of NWO Hollywood interfered and attacked both men.

The feud with Hogan and Rodman placed Page on the national stage. Rodman and Hogan appeared on *The Tonight Show with Jay Leno* in order to talk about Page. During the interview, Karl Malone of the Utah Jazz walked out with Page. *The Tonight Show* set nearly turned into a wrestling ring. A few days later, WCW signed Hogan and Rodman to wrestle Page and Malone in the main event of Bash at the Beach on July 12, 1998, in San Diego, California.

The presence of the NBA stars made Hogan and Rodman vs. Page and Malone one of the most anticipated matches in wrestling history. WCW gave credentials to hundreds of members of the national media for the match. Of course, Hogan, who had been the sport's greatest star for two decades, was used to the attention, as were the two NBA players. But Page had never received so much attention. For him, this was like the World Series and the Super Bowl combined.

Rodman and Hogan kept Malone and Page off-balance for most of the match, and they dictated the pace. Then Page tagged Malone, who dropped Rodman and Hogan to the mat with a series of clotheslines and bodyslams. Page tagged in and nearly finished off Hogan with a Diamond cutter. But then, as Rodman and Malone battled in the ring, the Disciple interfered and executed his apocalypse finisher on DDP. Then he rolled Hogan on top of Page for the pin. Malone complained to the referee, but his words fell on deaf ears.

"That Malone's the biggest crybaby I've ever heard," Hogan said. "We beat them in the middle of the ring. Nobody can beat Hollywood and Rodzilla with the Disciple watching our backs!"

On *Nitro* the next night, NWO Hollywood again attacked Page, injuring his leg. A week later, Page was barely able to wrestle in his match against Bret Hart for the vacant U.S. title. Hart won easily, and afterward Page vowed revenge against Hogan.

But NWO Hollywood—especially Eric Bischoff—had turned their attention to talk show host Jay Leno. Bischoff and Hogan made fun of Leno's jutting chin and *The Tonight Show.* Bischoff started doing a talk show segment of his own on *Nitro* broadcasts, segments clearly meant to insult Leno and *The Tonight Show.*

Leno answered back during his weeknight monologues. Page also stepped to Leno's side.

"I got his back," Page declared.

WCW couldn't resist pairing Page and Leno against Bischoff and Hogan at the Road Wild pay-per-view event on August 9 in Sturgis, South Dakota. For weeks before the match, Page trained both Leno and bandleader, Kevin Eubanks. On match night, Leno stepped into the ring ready to wrestle. Again, hundreds of members of the national media were present.

Early on in the match, Leno threw water at Hogan and Bischoff. As the match went on, Leno proved that he had some wrestling ability as he exhibited such holds as armlocks and arm twists. Late in the match, Leno delivered a low blow on Bischoff. Eubanks bounded into the ring and used a Diamond cutter on Bischoff. Leno pounced onto Bischoff and scored the pin. Bischoff and Hogan went after Leno, but WCW world champion Bill Goldberg got in their way. It was a horribly embarrassing loss for Hogan and Bischoff, and a big win for Page and Leno.

This gimmick tag team match involving NBA stars and talk show hosts had distracted Page from his real goal: winning championships. DDP got back on track at Fall Brawl '98, when he won the War Games battle royal to earn a shot at the WCW world champion. Page battled world champion Bill Goldberg at Halloween Havoc and nearly won with his Diamond cutter when Goldberg's shoulder was injured. But Goldberg, ever resilient, won the match with a spear and a jackhammer.

Rather than being down after the loss, DDP bounced back the next night and beat Hart for his second WCW U.S. title. Page feuded with Hart after Hart attacked him with a chair. At World War III, Hart used a DDT, a Russian legsweep, and a figure-four leglock on Page. DDP countered with a sharpshooter and a Diamond cutter to regain the U.S. title in the main event. But the relentless Hart recaptured the title from Page on

Though he eventually lost the bout, DDP gave superstar Bill Goldberg a run for his money at WCW's Halloween Havoc.

November 30, 1998, thanks to the Giant's interference. Next week at *Nitro*, the Giant chokeslammed DDP through a wooden table.

Page's feuds with Hart and the hated Giant made him more popular than ever. His popularity was increasing outside the ring, too. In December, DDP held his Reading, Rock, and Wrestling Holiday Weekend Extravaganza in Asbury Park, New Jersey. Page joined with Scholastic Books, as well as rock star Jon Bon Jovi and actor Chaz Palminteri, to

> **"I want to reach out and try to help other kids who have similar problems or those who don't have access to a lot of books."**
>
> **-Diamond Dallas Page, on dyslexia**

create a program that encouraged children to read.

"I had dyslexia when I was a kid," Page said. "It took a long time before it was diagnosed and some teachers just wrote me off as being stupid. It really tore me up inside. I want to reach out and try to help other kids who have similar problems or those who don't have access to a lot of books."

By the time Page used his Diamond cutter to beat the Giant at Starrcade on December 27, 1998, he had guaranteed that one day, there'd be a section in wrestling history books all about him.

# 8 Turning the Page

The reunion of the NWO at Starrcade '98 did nothing to slow DDP. Instead, it made him a more determined man. But as long as Kimberly was by his side, DDP would always be a distracted man, too.

Scott Steiner knew that the best way to get DDP's attention was to insult Kimberly, so that's exactly what he did. The result was a hot feud between DDP and the muscleman who called himself Big Poppa Pump.

Scott Steiner and Page wrestled at SuperBrawl '99. The rules were that if Steiner won, he'd get Kimberly for thirty days. Page seemed on his way to victory when Buff Bagwell interfered. Steiner placed Page in his Steiner recliner finishing hold and DDP passed out in pain. Steiner had Kimberly.

DDP was dead set on revenge, but new WCW president Ric Flair got in his way. Flair's interference prevented Page from beating Steiner. Page complained. To the fans, however, it sounded as if he was whining. Suddenly, and for no apparent reason, the fans had switched sides in the Steiner vs. Page feud. Steiner had become the fan favorite. Now Page was the bad guy.

With the referee knocked out cold, fans howl with anticipation as **DDP** and Kevin Nash stare each other down outside the ring.

DDP was shocked. He couldn't believe that the fans had turned against him, but he was determined to show them that they were wrong. Page, Hogan, Sting, and Flair battled in a four-way match for Flair's WCW world title at Spring Stampede on April 11, 1999. DDP eliminated Hogan early in the match. Sting dropped Page to the canvas. Then Randy Savage interfered and attacked both Flair and Sting. The three wrestlers were on their backs. The referee started to count them out. But at the nine count, Page got up, executed a Diamond cutter on Flair, and scored the pin. DDP was the new world champion. And he didn't care how he had won. The new WCW world champion was now the most hated man in the federation.

DDP turns the tables on Ric Flair, who has Page's partner, Sting, in a sleeperhold.

Page lost the world title to Sting on April 26, 1999, but regained the belt later the same night. Two weeks later, he lost the belt to Nash. DDP also formed the Triad with Bam Bam Bigelow and Kanyon and teamed with both men to win the world tag team belts. He formed an alliance with Savage, his former enemy, and feuded with Goldberg and Flair.

Kimberly entered the spotlight again in August 1999, when wrestler Billy Kidman revealed during an interview that she was his favorite Nitro Girl. Page attacked Kidman several times, as Kimberly hopelessly tried to stop him. But Page was uncontrollable. One night on *Thunder*, he challenged Sting, Goldberg, and Hogan to matches. At Fall Brawl '99, Goldberg pinned Page, who later interfered in the main event between Hogan and Sting.

On *Nitro* the next night, Page helped Sting and Luger beat Hogan and Bret Hart. A week later, Page saved Sting and Luger from an attack by Flair. At Halloween Havoc, Page used David Flair's (Ric Flair's son) crowbar to beat Ric Flair. But the next night, David Flair used the crowbar on Page, who had to be taken to a hospital. Now Page was feuding with both Flairs. Page also had a falling out with both Luger and Sting. The new DDP was fighting battles on all fronts. He battled David Flair in a Crowbar on a Pole match at Starrcade '99. DDP won with a Diamond cutter.

Page's personal life started overshadowing his wrestling life. Rumors circulated that Buff Bagwell was having an affair with Kimberly. Page confronted Bagwell, and the two had a heated brawl that was stopped by security guards. Page demanded a match against Bagwell. Bagwell started making offensive remarks about Kimberly, claiming that "all of the wrestlers had seen her birthmark." Page and Bagwell battled in a no rules, no referee, last man standing match at Souled Out on January 16, 2000. The two men battled all over the arena, brutalizing each other with foreign objects. Bagwell won, but when Kimberly walked to ringside, Page attacked him from behind.

Diamond Dallas Page lands a punch on an opponent.

But DDP had to wonder: Was something going on between his wife and Bagwell? Kimberly was the guest referee for a match between the two men. When Page used his Diamond cutter to pin Bagwell, Kimberly left the ring instead of joining her husband's celebration.

The feud, however, was cut short when Page suffered a back injury. The fans didn't see him again until *Nitro* on March 27, 2000, when he discussed his film, *Ready to Rumble*, and declared his intentions to become a three-time world champion. The next month, Page beat Sting in the finals of a four-man tournament to determine who would battle world champion Jeff Jarrett at Spring Stampede.

Page vs. Jarrett at Spring Stampede was an outstanding match. The advantage switched several times, and Page even escaped Jarrett's figure-four leglock. Kimberly came to the ring holding a guitar. It looked as if she was going to slug Jarrett, but instead she smashed the guitar over Page's head. Jarrett covered Page for the pin. After the match, Jarrett, Kimberly, and Eric Bischoff—the leader of the New Blood—hugged.

Page was shocked. The next night, Kimberly told the fans that Page was a glory hog. A week later, Kimberly declared that she wanted a divorce. Page was enraged. He attacked Bischoff, but Jarrett nailed him with a guitar. Later that night, Page battled Jarrett for the world title. Page scored with a Diamond cutter, then covered Jarrett for the pin. He had become a three-time WCW world champion. But not for long. DDP lost the title a few nights later in a tag team match pinning him and actor David Arquette against Jarrett and Bischoff. Because of an unusual technicality, when Arquette pinned Bischoff, Arquette became the new world champion.

At Slamboree 2000, Jarrett regained the world title in a three-way match involving Page and Arquette. The next night on *Nitro*, while Page was battling Mike O. Awesome, Kimberly again showed up with the divorce papers and asked Page to sign them. Awesome powerbombed Page through a table and forced him to sign the papers. Page was taken away on a stretcher.

Page was heartsick. He seemed to have lost Kimberly. He took out his frustrations on Awesome, but that didn't make him feel any better. Kimberly got a restraining order against DDP and removed his belongings from their house.

At the Great American Bash, Kimberly whacked DDP with a lead pipe.

Distraught, Page grabbed a microphone, and told the fans that wrestling had cost him his health, his friends, and his wife. Then he walked out of the ring and into the crowd. Had wrestling seen the last of DDP?

The answer was no. On November 6, on *Nitro*, DDP made his return to the ring and pledged his allegiance to the fans. Wrestling had been a part of his life since the late 1980s, and it would continue to be a part of his life.

"You love me, you hate me, you'll never forget me," DDP loves to say. Truer words have never been spoken.

# Glossary

**brass knuckles match**  Special type of match in which both wrestlers wear brass knuckles on their hands.

**clique**  Small, exclusive group of people; for example, in pro wrestling, the New World Order and the NWO Wolfpac.

**Diamond cutter**  Finishing maneuver in which the opponent is held in place by the neck over the wrestler's shoulder, and is then dragged down violently, face first, onto the floor.

**disqualification**   Ruling by the referee in which a wrestler automatically loses a match for violating a rule.

**draw**   In wrestling, a match in which neither wrestler wins; a tie.

**feud**   Series of matches between two wrestlers or two tag teams. Frequently, one wrestler will bad-mouth the other wrestler or will sneak attack the wrestler.

**foreign object**   Illegal object used in the ring, such as a chair or a pencil.

**main event**  The featured match at a wrestling show, usually the last match of the night.

**pin**  When either both shoulders or both shoulder blades are held in contact with the mat for three continuous seconds. A pin ends a match.

**pinfall**  Win achieved by a pin.

**rulebreaker**  In wrestling, a bad guy; generally someone disliked by the fans. So-called because he often violates the rulebook.

**scientific match**  Match between two or more wrestlers in which the combatants rely mostly on amateur wrestling moves, rather than kicking and punching.

**small package**  Counter-wrestling move in which the wrestler being pinned grabs the opponent's legs or upper body, rolls him over, and into pinning position.

**submission hold**  Move that makes an opponent give up without being pinned.

**submission match**  Special match in which the only way to win is by forcing your opponent to submit.

**tag team match**  Match involving two teams of two or more wrestlers. Only one wrestler from each team is allowed in the ring at a time.

**technical wrestler**   Professional wrestler who uses basic amateur wrestling moves and tries to win matches by out-thinking and out-wrestling the opponent, rather than by wearing him down with kicks and punches.

**turnbuckle**   The padded corners of a wrestling ring where the ropes meet.

# For More Information

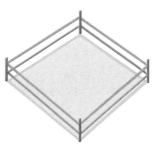

## Magazines

*Pro Wrestling Illustrated, The Wrestler, Inside Wrestling, Wrestle America,* and *Wrestling Superstars*
London Publishing Co.
7002 West Butler Pike
Ambler, PA 19002

*WCW Magazine*
P.O. Box 420235
Palm Coast, FL 32142-0235

## WOW *Magazine*

McMillen Communications
P.O. Box 500
Missouri City, TX 77459-9904

# Web Sites

Professional Wrestling Online Museum
http://www.wrestlingmuseum.com

Pro Wrestling Torch newsletter
http://www.pwtorch.com

World Championship Wrestling
http://www.wcw.com

World Wrestling Federation
http://www.wwf.com

# Works Cited

"America's Wrestler: Taking a Page from the Dallas Playbook." *The Wrestler Presents True Life Stories*, Summer 1998, pp. 16–25.

Anderson, Steve. "DDP's Ph.D: Earning His Degree in Grappology." *The Wrestler*, March 1997, pp. 66–69.

Rosenbaum, Dave. "Diamond Dallas Page Strikes Gold: Now He's the Target of the NWO and WCW!" *Inside Wrestling Digest*, Spring 1998, pp. 79–81.

"Stripped of Their Dignity: Can Kimberly & DDP Ever Recover?" *The Wrestler*, August 1997, pp. 42–45.

# For Further Reading

Albano, Lou, Bert Randolph Sugar, and Michael
    Benson. *The Complete Idiot's Guide to
    Pro Wrestling*. 2nd ed. New York: Alpha
    Books, 2000.

Myers, Robert. *The Professional Wrestling
    Trivia Book*. Boston, MA: Branden
    Books, 1999.

Page, Diamond Dallas. *Positively Page: The
    Diamond Dallas Page Journey*.
    Baltimore, MD: Positive Publications, 2000.

# Index

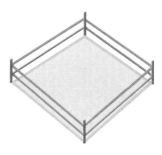

# Photo Credits

Cover and interior shots by Colin Bowman.

# Series Design and Layout

Geri Giordano